FOLLOW ME!

Transforming and shaping
lives for the journey

ALI CAMPBELL

**kevin
mayhew**

kevin
mayhew

First published in Great Britain in 2018 by Kevin Mayhew Ltd
Buxhall, Stowmarket, Suffolk IP14 3BW
Tel: +44 (0) 1449 737978 Fax: +44 (0) 1449 737834
E-mail: info@kevinmayhew.com

www.kevinmayhew.com

9 8 7 6 5 4 3 2 1 0

ISBN 978 1 84867 954 2
Catalogue No. 1501580

Cover design by Rob Mortonson
© Image used under licence from Shutterstock Inc.
Edited by Linda Ottewell
Typeset by Angela Selfe

Printed and bound in Great Britain

Contents

About the author

Ali is married to the lovely Lisa and has two amazing daughters, Hannah and Ellie. When not hanging out with his family (in a caravan or going on adventure walks or discovering the delights of the North West of England), Ali works as a children's and youth ministry consultant, seeking to equip and encourage the local church in its work with young people. Over the last 32 years, Ali has been a volunteer youth worker, a youth minister at a parish church, worked for a Church of England Diocese and been involved in hosting camps and conferences for children and young people.

Ali's passion to see young people discover who Jesus is and live life to the full in relationship with him has led to this book.

In praise of Follow Me

Follow Me is an engaging resource which will enhance the spiritual lives of young people in the church. Readers are invited to go on an explorative journey through 40 concise chapters that are rich with knowledge and reliable stories. The *Follow Me* symbols make it accessible and user-friendly for any young people, enabling them to engage in reflective practice about their own spiritual journey. Through relevant modern-day examples and strong theological insight, *Follow Me* is an essential resource for any teenage Christian.

Liz Edge, Youth Work Practitioner

Ali's heart, to put the voices and lives of young people at the heart of our engagement with them, has yielded this great resource. Creative, informative and full of wisdom it stems from his many years of experience working alongside young people and enabling discipleship, centring on a passion for Jesus and a commitment to Scripture. I can't wait to use it with my own nurture group and am sure the depth of material here will keep us pondering far beyond the 40 days!

Alice Smith, Lead Tutor for Theology and Youth Ministry,
St Mellitus College

This is a generation in desperate need of relentless love, rock-solid truth and game-changing role models. Engaging in *Follow Me* will warm the bones, strengthen spiritual muscles and captivate young people with the compelling person and message of Jesus. It is punchy, fun, innovative and inspiring. It will change the lives of all who throw themselves into it.

Phil Knox, Head of Mission to Young Adults, Evangelical Alliance

Deep thinking and really relevant ideas that will help young people get to grip with what it means to give their all in pursuit of Jesus.

Rachel Gardner, Director of National Work at Youthscape,
President of Girls Brigade England and Wales

Introduction

There's a host of great characters in the Bible but they can sometimes make us feel inadequate! They do amazing stuff for God with incredible faith, courage and strength. From prophets to kings, people that inspire but are also slightly terrifying! I think that is why I love Peter, one of Jesus' disciples. This guy also does amazing stuff but he can also be a bit of a donut, both saying and doing things that just feel a bit more like, well, me. IF I had been one of Jesus' first disciples and IF I had been the main source for one of the books of the Bible – it is reckoned that the Gospel of Mark was mostly based on conversations with Peter – I would have airbrushed out my stuff-ups, my silly bits, the times I didn't get it and had no idea what Jesus was up to. Peter leaves it all in there; it is part of his story. All of it, the good and the bad, is part of his journey of faith as he follows Jesus.

In these devotions we are going to look at who Jesus is, what he has done for us, and the life we can have through him. As we encounter Peter we'll look at conversations he had with Jesus, what he did when Jesus died, what he did when the Holy Spirit came, how he lived his life after Jesus had risen from the dead – still with times where he didn't get it and made mistakes – as the early Church began.

Jesus loves YOU. Warts and all. Jesus wants you to follow him, with all that you are. So, as we journey with Jesus bring the whole of yourself along. Let's see how he can transform us and shape our lives for the journey – just as he did with Peter.

Follow Me Symbols

The first thing Jesus says to Peter is 'Follow me', and it is where we will begin. What follows are 40 devotions with a Bible passage, a bit of reflection and then some things for you to do and think about if you want to. The symbols below will appear after each bit of Scripture and guide you through the reflection.

 When you look at a map you don't just see the bit you want to get to. Everything around that bit gives you context and a sense of place. It's the same with the Bible. If the space next to the map icon is blank – YOU think about what else is going on as you read round the verse for the day. Why is this happening now? What else is going on? Sometimes I might lob in something interesting about the context that makes it clearer what is happening and why.

 What particular thing is being lit up by this verse? Maybe a theme for our lives, maybe a key thing about Jesus, the gospel, our journey.

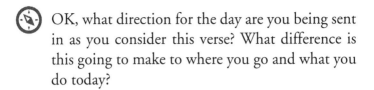 OK, what direction for the day are you being sent in as you consider this verse? What difference is this going to make to where you go and what you do today?

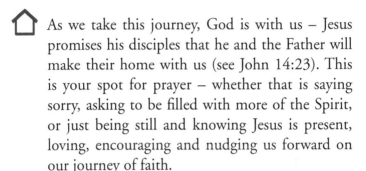 As we take this journey, God is with us – Jesus promises his disciples that he and the Father will make their home with us (see John 14:23). This is your spot for prayer – whether that is saying sorry, asking to be filled with more of the Spirit, or just being still and knowing Jesus is present, loving, encouraging and nudging us forward on our journey of faith.

Day 1

*When he had finished speaking, he said to Simon,
'Put out into deep water, and let down the nets for
a catch.' Simon answered, 'Master, we've worked
hard all night and haven't caught anything. But
because you say so, I will let down the nets.'*

Luke 5:4, 5

I don't know about you, but I struggle with being
told what to do. This is especially true if I know best!
I don't know what went through Peter's mind here, if
he struggled to answer, paused and then said it politely
but through gritted teeth, or had been so blown away
by what Jesus had been saying he would have done
anything this man asked. Yet Peter was a fisherman. It
was his thing. Do you have something like that, your
thing? Imagine someone came along who didn't know
about music, maths, art, football, collecting furry frogs,
looking after pets, bicycles or running and they told you
a 'better way' of doing your thing? What would you do?

 At the beginning of this chapter the crowd is
pressing up against Jesus, desperate to hear what
he is saying. I don't know if he was literally being
backed towards the lake of Galilee, but he hops
into a boat and asks to be put out a bit from the
shore. The fishermen have done their work, they

are finished, sitting on the shore washing their nets. They have caught nothing. Jesus sits down, which might seem odd if there are a bunch of people on the shore trying to get a look at him and listen, but sitting down was a sign from a rabbi (a teacher) that they were about to teach. The crowd would have hushed, the fishermen were sitting in the boat – a captive audience – and wow, what Jesus said must have captured their hearts!

 Peter says to Jesus, 'Because you say so, I will . . .' You aren't the fisherman here, I am – but ok.

 In our lives today, where do we think we have it all sorted or are the expert? Maybe there are things we have been trying that aren't working. Maybe Jesus says to us, 'Put out into deep water' and we might be like, 'I've done that already!' Do we need to say, as we start together, 'Because you say so, I will'?

 Lord Jesus, help me to discover more about your love, your power and your presence in my life through these times together.
Amen.

Day 2

*'Come follow me,' Jesus said, 'and I will
make you fishers of men.' At once they left
their nets and followed him.*

Mark 1:17, 18

The invitation to follow is not just random here. The invitation has a purpose. On MTV there is a reality TV show called *Made*. It's been running since 2002 and each season a bunch of young people appear who want their life 'made' into the one they have always dreamed of – triathlete, boxer, lifeguard, cheerleader . . . It's about taking what is and then transforming it. Jesus looks at these guys and says, 'Let me make you . . . I know you have been doing this, but here is THIS for you, come and join me!' And they do.

 As well as offering a greater purpose in life for these two men than fishing, Jesus has also laid out God's plan and hope for all of us in what he says just before this in verse 15: 'The kingdom of God is near. Repent and believe the good news.' To *repent* is literally to turn about and head in a new direction.

 'At once.' No hesitation, no apparent packing up and even putting their nets away. They left it all, at once. Is there anything God is asking you to do straight away? At once?

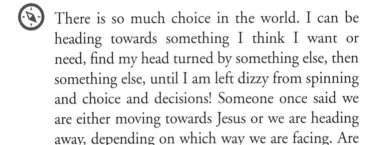 There is so much choice in the world. I can be heading towards something I think I want or need, find my head turned by something else, then something else, until I am left dizzy from spinning and choice and decisions! Someone once said we are either moving towards Jesus or we are heading away, depending on which way we are facing. Are you turned towards him today?

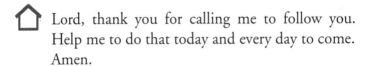 Lord, thank you for calling me to follow you. Help me to do that today and every day to come. Amen.

Day 3

While Jesus was still speaking, some people came from the house of Jairus, the synagogue ruler. 'Your daughter is dead,' they said. 'Why bother the teacher any more?' Ignoring what they said, Jesus told the synagogue ruler, 'Don't be afraid; just believe.' He did not let anyone follow him except Peter, James and John.

Mark 5:35-37

Here is another invitation! So far in following Jesus (yes, I know this is only day 3 for us!), Peter has witnessed Jesus' own family thinking he has lost the plot, seen healing, been struck by how big the crowds are getting, watched as Jesus calmed a storm, restored a possessed man and now, here he is among the select few taken by Jesus to see something else that is incredible.

 Since Jairus has told Jesus about his sick daughter, Jesus has been held up by the needs of someone else. He stops when he realises someone has touched him (Mark 5:30). To make matters worse he then hangs around looking through the crowd to see who it is (verse 32). Jairus must be going NUTS. Imagine what he is thinking. Why has Jesus stopped? What is he doing? So what if power left him, my daughter needs him NOW! Jesus had a ministry of interruptions and if you read on, you'll discover that Jairus' daughter IS healed. How hard it is to wait sometimes! How hard it is to set off and then get held up! Maybe others come in on your journey with Jesus and say to you, 'Don't bother.' Can you keep their voices still and listen to Jesus?

 'Don't be afraid; just believe.' Do you know what the most common command is in the Bible? You might think it would be a command to 'do' something. Go and do this, go and do that, but it is a don't. Not a finger wagging, telling you off, what on earth did you think you were doing kind of 'don't', but a reassuring, 'I am with you, don't be AFRAID.'

 When we struggle to believe, our lives can get out of kilter, we can worry, be anxious, lose perspective. What is amazing about Jesus – and Peter gets to witness so much of his earthly life – is how, in the midst of being the Word of God made flesh, the Son who has come to bring life, hope and peace for the whole world, in the midst of all that, Jesus still cared about the individuals who were with him. Peter, James, John, you and me. We might not feel we are lifted out of our places of fear and worry straight away but let's just believe, just trust and just know that Jesus is with us.

This is your space. There is a lot in this short passage, what strikes you? What do you know you need to pray about or pray for after reading it? Be quiet, be still. Bring your cares and your worries to Jesus. Don't be afraid.

Day 4

*When Jesus came into Peter's house, he saw
Peter's mother-in-law lying in bed with a fever.
He touched her hand and the fever left her,
and she got up and began to wait on him.*

Matthew 8:14, 15

Everything in Peter's life is open to Jesus. Imagine, Jesus
is chatting to you and walking along with you and he
suddenly says, 'Let's go to your house.' Are you thrilled?
Are you going white at the thought, as you think
of the absolute STATE of your room? (The food under
the bed that is going to walk off by itself soon, your
clothes thrown around the place, the unmade bed, the
embarrassing pictures on the wall from when you liked
that band when you were 8 . . .) Nothing is off limits.
It is perfectly natural for a rabbi (a teacher, as we have
mentioned that Jesus is) to literally share the whole of
their lives, space, living together, eating together, the
whole deal. Does Jesus have your EVERYTHING?
Every space, nook, corner and room of your life?

 What you notice as you read around this passage
is that Jesus is constantly on the move. Jesus might
share life and space with his disciples, but there is
nowhere that is fully his home on earth. Hospitality
in Jesus' time was pretty amazing. Houses were

open to guests, to strangers turning up in a village, to new people, to those without a place to stay. It was pretty normal stuff to be looked after in this way. It was pretty normal too for a rabbi to travel a lot and NOT have a settled place.

 'She got up and began to wait on him.' In the midst of all this moving around, going from place to place, never still, constantly in demand (straight after this passage it seems a crowd descend on the house looking for Jesus to heal and comfort them), we have the response of this woman. As soon as she is healed and out of bed, her focus is Jesus. She serves Jesus, she looks to Jesus' needs. This woman waited on him. If Jesus does something stonking for you, what is your reaction? Wait on him, or get on with your life?

 Waiting is a part of our following Jesus. Not EVERYTHING is about living life on fast forward, going from place to place doing and seeing amazing things. We need to take stock, we need to wait, we need to wait on Jesus. Sometimes I can run off busily, doing 'good' things, but not necessarily doing 'God' things.

 Wait right now. Don't rush off. Yes, the day is about to happen, or you are about to nod off rather than rush off (if you are doing these notes at the other end of the day . . . or in a boring lesson at school). Wait. Give space to God to speak to you right now.

Day 5

From this time many of his disciples turned back and no longer followed him. 'You do not want to leave too, do you?' Jesus asked the Twelve. Simon Peter answered him, 'Lord, to whom shall we go? You have the words of eternal life. We believe and know that you are the Holy One of God.'

John 6:66-69

Life is not a popularity contest. There are some tough calls to make as we grow and discover more about ourselves and who we want to be – and more about Jesus and who he calls us to be. Sometimes we wrestle with ourselves, other times we can struggle if our friends don't love Jesus and don't want to follow him. But when we hold on to what we know to be true, our true friends will still be there.

 This might be surprising – some people are starting to leave Jesus. This is the man who we have just said is surrounded by crowds, people are in awe and captivated by what he is doing, but they are beginning to be challenged by what he is saying. Jesus came to change everything. In the previous bit of chapter 6, Jesus talks about being the 'bread of life', likening himself to the bread from heaven that fed the Israelites when they wandered through the desert. Only, Jesus' body and blood will bring eternal life – not relieving a moment of physical hunger but changing EVERYTHING. Some couldn't handle this news, couldn't take it in. This is, after all, only Joseph's son – how can this be?

'You have the words of eternal life.' When you find someone, or something, that brings life and hope, you don't give it up easily! More than that, Peter has realised they have fully thrown everything in with Jesus. If this isn't it, what else is there?! Maybe that is where his, 'to whom shall we go?' comes from.

It can be hard to hold on to the truth of who Jesus is – and what he offers each of us. LIFE. Eternal life! There might be those around us who cannot see it, can't believe it to be true. Struggle with it. Have you, like Peter, thrown your lot in with Jesus? Peter says two things after recognising that Jesus has the words of eternal life. He says we have come to 'believe' and to 'know'. Peter believes who Jesus is, and he has also begun to know him. We can believe that Jesus is Lord, but do we know him as Lord of our lives?

Someone once said that Jesus is 'Lord of all' or he is not Lord at all. Meaning, we can't just give him a part of ourselves. Following Jesus really is a bit like what Peter and those early disciples did, leaving everything for Jesus' sake. When you feel that tug to leave Jesus, is it really that there are things that you don't want to let go of?

Day 6

Peter said, 'Explain the parable to us.' 'Are you still so dull?' Jesus asked them. 'Don't you see that whatever enters the mouth goes into the stomach and then out of the body? But the things that come out of a person's mouth come from the heart, and these defile them.'

Matthew 15:15-18

Have you ever had something you thought was true completely turned on its head? That is what happens here to the disciples. They are trying to get their heads round what Jesus has just said – it kind of blows out of the water what they have been taught by the religious leaders of Jesus' day. Poor Peter, he asks what everyone else is thinking and *Boom* – they all get a smack down!

 Jesus has been criticised at the beginning of this chapter – his disciples have been told off for not washing their hands! Ritual, especially around physical cleanliness, was just what you did. It had become more than a symbol of needing to be clean on the inside, it had replaced it! Doing the right 'outward' things had become enough for the religious leaders, and it is what they taught and practised. They had forgotten something God told Samuel, hundreds of years earlier, 'God looks at the heart' (1 Samuel 16:7). We can look great on the outside but be rotten on the inside.

'The things that come out of a person's mouth come from the heart.' What comes out of your mouth? Do you bless others, do you think before you speak?

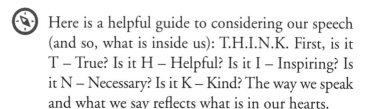

Here is a helpful guide to considering our speech (and so, what is inside us): T.H.I.N.K. First, is it T – True? Is it H – Helpful? Is it I – Inspiring? Is it N – Necessary? Is it K – Kind? The way we speak and what we say reflects what is in our hearts.

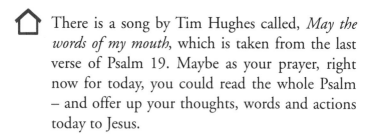

There is a song by Tim Hughes called, *May the words of my mouth*, which is taken from the last verse of Psalm 19. Maybe as your prayer, right now for today, you could read the whole Psalm – and offer up your thoughts, words and actions today to Jesus.

Day 7

*Jesus and his disciples went on to the villages
around Caesarea Philippi. On the way he asked
them, 'Who do people say I am?' They replied,
'Some say John the Baptist; others say Elijah;
and still others, one of the prophets.' 'But what
about you?' he asked. 'Who do you say I am?
Peter answered, 'You are the Messiah.'*

Mark 8:27-29

I grew up 'knowing' Jesus. All my life I have gone to church, but I hit a point when I had to ask myself, 'Do I believe this? Is this real? Is this true? Do I know Jesus?' Until I started asking these questions, I realised I had done what the disciples say at the beginning of this passage – when the disciples say who other people think Jesus is. I could answer, 'Well, my youth leader says this, my Mum says this, my brother says this, the church leader says this . . .'. What other people think and say is not what Jesus is after!

 As you read the Gospels, especially Matthew, Mark and Luke, you will discover very similar bits of Scripture. Not quite the same, but near enough. This passage has echoes of the one we looked at yesterday. In Mark's Gospel, right up until this point in almost every chapter, people have been asking, 'Who is Jesus? WHO IS JESUS!!' The reference to Elijah and John the Baptist might seem odd, but Elijah was taken up to heaven and didn't 'die' an earthly death. Some believed that when Elijah returned, it would be God's kingdom come on earth, others thought John the Baptist *was* Elijah returned . . . So, these were the names being chucked about as Jesus was being mentioned and discussed and the crowds witnessed the miracles and heard his teaching.

'Who do you say I am?' This is probably the most important question in the history of the world. The answer to it has MASSIVE implications! Think about that for a minute – who is Jesus to you? What does it mean to know him? What difference does knowing him make?

Are you a chameleon? By that I mean do you change who you are and what you think depending on who you are hanging out with? Drifting from one way of being to another – or, do you know who you are and what you think? It can be tough! It can be about our confidence, whether we consider what we know and believe to be worth anything – but it can also be about who we put our confidence in. I have friends and family but, of everyone I know, I have found only Jesus is constant, sure, faithful all the time, and totally trustworthy. I might shift a lot and be wobbly with my faith and who I am sometimes, but Jesus is not. Who will you put your trust in?

 Maybe take some time here. Be still and imagine Jesus looking at you and asking you, 'Who do you say I am?' What would you say, what could you pray?

Day 8

*'But what about you?' he asked. 'Who do you say I
am?' Simon Peter answered, 'You are the Messiah, the
Son of the living God.' Jesus replied, 'Blessed are you,
Simon son of Jonah, for this was not revealed to you by
flesh and blood, but by my Father in heaven.'*

Matthew 16:15-17

This is WHY I love Peter! On day 6 we had Peter
opening his mouth, only to have all the disciples called
'dull' because they didn't get what Jesus was talking
about. It doesn't stop Peter. He comes back, again and
again – as we will see through his journey with Jesus.
Whoops, then straight back at it; HUGE mess up, back
he comes again. He never gives up on pressing in to
grasp and know and love Jesus.

 From here on in, especially in Matthew and
Mark, Jesus makes it clearer and clearer where
everything is heading. To Jerusalem, to fulfil his
mission, to bring about the salvation of the world.
It is big stuff. The biggest. With his answer to the
question, 'Who am I?' Peter gets it bang on. There
is no indication here that Peter realises *how* he
knows what he knows about Jesus when he makes
his statement – but is so clear and so right – Jesus
knows. Peter has heard from God.

'You are the Messiah, the Son of the living God.' Messiah literally means *anointed one*, someone who is set apart for a special purpose. In Greek that word is *Christos*, which is where we get *Christ* from.

 We don't need to have a perfect understanding or know a whole bunch of stuff from the Bible really well before we can say *yes* to Jesus and follow him for ourselves. Peter didn't, and he put his complete trust and faith in Jesus.

 What does it mean for Jesus to be the Messiah? What does it mean for Jesus to be *your* Messiah. Think about that, ask God to show you how to live for the Messiah today.

Day 9

*'And I tell you that you are Peter, and on this rock
I will build my church, and the gates of Hades
will not overcome it. I will give you the keys of the
kingdom of heaven; whatever you bind on earth
will be bound in heaven, and whatever you loose
on earth will be loosed in heaven.'*

Matthew 16:18, 19

I think Peter got more than he bargained for here! He gets a bit of a name change – from Simon Peter to an emphasis on the Peter. Then some pretty staggering words are spoken over him by Jesus – look what can happen when we see who Jesus is!

 At the beginning of Matthew chapter 16 there is the demand for a sign from Jesus that he is who he says he is. By the time we get to the end of chapter 16 we have Jesus predicting his death. The cross has become the most recognised symbol and sign in the world. This was not the kind of sign the religious teachers had in mind.

 'You are Peter.' That is a really short bit of the above verses to focus on, but something really important has happened that has HUGE implications for you and me. Peter discovers who Jesus is (and who he is going to be) after he acknowledges who Jesus is.

'I don't know who you think you are!' Has this ever been said to you? Maybe you have done something silly, been extremely rude to a parent, taken something for granted, been ungrateful ... but, have you ever thought about it. Who are you? Really? What is your purpose? Peter thought he was destined to be a fisherman – nope. Jesus had other plans; Jesus knew Peter better than Peter knew himself. He knows you, too.

 When we acknowledge Jesus as our Messiah, we begin to discover who we are. Jesus has plans and purposes for us, that are part of what he is growing and building and doing in this world through his followers. We are invited, along with Peter, to join in! How might Jesus ask you to join in with bringing his light and life into the world today?

Day 10

*From that time on Jesus began to explain to his
disciples that he must go to Jerusalem and suffer
many things at the hands of the elders, the chief
priests and teachers of the law, and that he must be
killed and on the third day be raised to life. Peter
took him aside and began to rebuke him. 'Never,
Lord!' he said. 'This shall never happen to you!'
Jesus turned and said to Peter, 'Get behind me,
Satan! You are a stumbling block to me; you do
not have in mind the concerns of God, but
merely human concerns.'*

Matthew 16:21-23

Peter, which means *rock*, has gone from being 'Rocky',
who Jesus is going to use in a mighty way, to a stone that
Jesus is going to trip over! What happened? Hero to zero
– has that ever happened to you? Mighty one minute,
missed it the next?

 A lot is going on here and just reading about it is
hard. What was Peter's tone of voice? What was
Jesus so disturbed about? It sounds as if Peter just
wants to protect his friend. There is a verse in the
Old Testament where God says, 'My thoughts are
not your thoughts, neither are your ways my ways'
(Isaiah 55:8). 'Messiah' to these first disciples,

including Peter, meant overthrowing the Romans, freeing the Jewish people again . . . it didn't mean death for Jesus!

 'You are a stumbling block to me.' This must have really stunned Peter, not what he was wanting at all. Sometimes we might mean well, and even do things with good intentions – but get in the way of what Jesus is doing.

 Do you ever say stuff before you have heard the whole of a story? Maybe you finish a joke for someone else (that is so annoying), maybe you think you know what someone is going to say, so if there is a pause you chip in. Sometimes we only hear half of what is said because we are so keen to get our voice heard and, as we get ready to speak, we stop listening. I don't know if that happened to Peter here. I think he has heard Jesus talk about suffering and death . . . and missed, completely missed, 'raised to life'!!

 We have a point of view. God has an infinite number of viewing points, for he sees everything. When we feel that we are stumbling or getting in the way of Jesus being good news through us, maybe we need to stop again and listen again. To be still, not rush in with what we have to say, but wait and see what Jesus has to say.

Day 11

Jesus took Peter, James and John with him and led them up a high mountain, where they were all alone. There he was transfigured before them. His clothes became dazzling white, whiter than anyone in the world could bleach them. And there appeared before them Elijah and Moses, who were talking with Jesus.

Mark 9:2-4

There are in life some defining moments – etched on your brain, living on in your memory – where everything is clear, bright and dazzling, as if it happened just now. Other things sometimes seem important but fade with time. They disappear from view and we struggle to picture the scene . . . What happened again? THIS was a once in a lifetime, never to be repeated event for Jesus' three closest friends – they had never seen, never IMAGINED anything like this!

 At the beginning of this chapter, just after Jesus has spoken about the way of the cross – he makes a statement about the kingdom of God coming with power – we then have this 'transfiguration' of Jesus on a mountain. He appears to be catching up with a couple of heroes from the Old Testament! The significance of these two? Moses represents the law, and for God's people at the time, he was their greatest leader ever. Elijah represents the prophets and one whose return would mean the kingdom was coming. And here they both are. With Jesus!

 'Where they were all alone.' This is sometimes referred to as a 'mountain-top' experience, because they were on a mountain (!) and it was pretty amazing. But, notice Jesus is not drawing HUGE attention to himself, he is not taking the platform in front of thousands. The disciples are not caught up in the thrill of an event with a crowd of adoring onlookers. They were all alone.

 Do we find that we encounter Jesus when we are in a crowd or by ourselves? What is your expectation about meeting with Jesus when you are all alone?

 Get yourself alone. Completely. Can you knock off the music, turn your phone to silent. Be still. Be totally alone with your own thoughts and with Jesus. You might not be on a mountain, but how does he appear to you? Be still, wait, watch, listen.

Day 12

Peter said to Jesus, 'Rabbi, it is good for us to be here. Let us put up three shelters – one for you, one for Moses and one for Elijah.' (He did not know what to say, they were so frightened.)

Mark 9:5, 6

Ahh. We have all had those moments. You know, an awkward silence, one of those pauses that just needs to be filled with words because it gets more and more uncomfortable the longer nobody is saying anything – or, you are up a mountain with your best friend and something totally bonkers beyond any frame of reference takes place and you just have to say something – anything!

 If you read the introduction at the front of this book, you'll remember that most scholars agree that Peter was the primary source for Mark's Gospel. The account of the transfiguration is also in Matthew's Gospel (Matthew is kind to Peter), and Luke's Gospel (Luke 9:33 quotes Peter and says, 'He did not know what he was saying.'). I love Peter's humility. He doesn't hide his weakness and fear. He could have just said, 'I was THERE!' and left everyone else jealous . . .

'He did not know what to say.' It is ok not to know what to say. It is all right. Sometimes we fill a silence with God with a load of babble. Maybe you have had a prayer time where you get to the end and you think, 'Well, THAT was a load of nonsense!' Not the act of praying, but your frustration with the words coming out of your mouth. We have all been there – Peter too.

 Not knowing what to say, think or do is part of the Christian life. What? Well, by ourselves we do not know – only with Jesus. We only rely on him when we cease to rely on ourselves. We cannot MAKE it as a Christian. We have to allow Jesus to shape and make us – after his image. We bring our whole selves to him – just as Peter did.

 When you pray, you do not need to say anything. There is this great bit that Paul writes in his letter to the Romans for when we do not know what to say. Read it here: Romans 8:26 – now pray!

Day 13

*While he was still speaking, a bright cloud covered
them, and a voice from the cloud said, 'This is my
Son, whom I love; with him I am well pleased. Listen
to him!' When the disciples heard this, they fell face
down to the ground, terrified. But Jesus came and
touched them. 'Get up,' he said. 'Don't be afraid.'
When they looked up, they saw no one except Jesus.*

Matthew 17:5-8

Lots of good things can distract us and draw our
attention – not just things that are bad – but, can we fix
our eyes and our hope on what is best?

 At Jesus' baptism there was a voice from heaven
saying the same thing – the only addition in this
passage is, 'Listen to him!'. In other places God,
through his Spirit, has met people, or an angel
has appeared and those present, like Peter and his
friends here, have been terrified. But also, as here,
these comforting words are said, 'Don't be afraid'.
There is a difference between an awe and wonder
kind of holy fear (this is GOD speaking!!) and
being terrified by some monster.

 'When they looked up, they saw no one except
Jesus.' In this most dramatic encounter of their

lives, what remains is not the cloud, not the booming voice, not the strange appearances of Moses and Elijah . . . but Jesus.

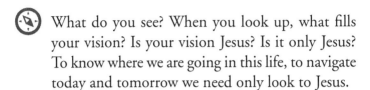

What do you see? When you look up, what fills your vision? Is your vision Jesus? Is it only Jesus? To know where we are going in this life, to navigate today and tomorrow we need only look to Jesus.

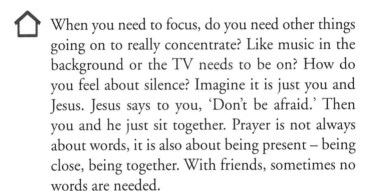

When you need to focus, do you need other things going on to really concentrate? Like music in the background or the TV needs to be on? How do you feel about silence? Imagine it is just you and Jesus. Jesus says to you, 'Don't be afraid.' Then you and he just sit together. Prayer is not always about words, it is also about being present – being close, being together. With friends, sometimes no words are needed.

Day 14

Jesus looked at them and said, 'With man this is impossible, but not with God; all things are possible with God.' Then Peter spoke up, 'We have left everything to follow you!' 'Truly I tell you', Jesus replied, 'no one who has left home or brothers or sisters or mother or father or children or fields for me and the gospel will fail to receive a hundred times as much in this present age.'

Mark 10:27-31

What has us in its grip? What can we not let go of? What hinders us as we try and follow Jesus?

 Read back a bit to before we get to this statement – what is it that is appearing impossible? Just before theses verses Jesus has seen a rich man go away disappointed. He had kept all the commandments but when Jesus said he needed to give away his riches, he went away sad. Jesus then says in verse 25, 'It is easier for a camel to go through the eye of a needle than for someone rich to enter the kingdom of God'. That conjures up a picture! The disciples were amazed on hearing these words because they had been taught that riches were a sign of God's blessing. If the rich will struggle then WHO stands a chance?

'All things are possible with God.' Something impossible is coming. Jesus knows what is coming, and has hope. He is heading towards the most incredible moment in history – when a man comes back from the dead – changing ALL that is possible. Changing everything for you and for me.

 For you and me it might not be riches (ha, I wish!). In the midst of his confusion about what Jesus is saying about riches, needles and camels – Peter can't cope! He cries out, 'We have left everything to follow you!' Jesus doesn't rebuke Peter; instead, Peter receives an encouragement. What we receive, though, is not riches as this world understands riches, but a family of brothers and sisters that stretches around the world, as we are part of God's family together and – through putting our trust in Jesus rather than anything else – life, life eternal!

 No matter how hard we try, there are always things that hinder – it is part of following Jesus – but, offer those things again today. Give them to Jesus, trust them to Jesus, whether they are thoughts, actions or words we find hard to let go of – with God, nothing is impossible!

Day 15

'What do you think, Simon?' he asked. 'From whom do the kings of the earth collect duty and taxes – from their own children or from others?' 'From others,' Peter answered. 'Then the children are exempt,' Jesus said to him. 'But so that we may not cause offence, go to the lake and throw out your line. Take the first fish you catch; open its mouth and you will find a four-drachma coin. Take it and give it to them for my tax and yours.'

Matthew 17:25-27

Being put on the spot is awkward. Yet being helped with the answer is amazing. Jesus does both here – he asks a question but helps Peter think through the answer. When we are on the spot, either with something we believe or something we are working out, we can know that Jesus will help us.

 Oh, there is loads happening in these couple of verses. The tax being discussed is the 'temple tax': a HUGE money spinner. For the people paying it, this was part of their 'atonement' for being sinners. The only place this story is mentioned is in Matthew's Gospel. Matthew had been a tax collector himself. Jesus makes a point here about his own sonship (He is the Son of God most High, so he shouldn't be paying a tax to the temple ...!)

 'What do you think?' I love this! Jesus does this a lot. He teaches his disciples not by TELLING them what is true and what is right and what to believe, but by asking them questions, getting them to think and contribute and reflect and wonder.

 Notice a couple of things – Jesus doesn't just pay his own tax (which he doesn't need to, being perfect), he also pays Peter's! It's a picture for us of what Jesus has done for each of us, by paying the price. Peter also gets told to go and fish, using a skill he has, so that Jesus can perform a miracle. We, you and I – get in on the act when Jesus is doing kingdom stuff. We are invited to get stuck in and make stuff happen – just like Peter.

 Here is something that Jesus doesn't need to do – but he does it. He doesn't want to be a stumbling block for Jews who would find it hard if their Messiah did not obey the law. We might not be in quite this situation but, with our faith and our life in God, maybe there are things that are not an issue for us. We have no problems with some challenges that face others. How generous or thoughtful are we of the needs and weaknesses of those around us?

Day 16

*Then Peter came to Jesus and asked, 'Lord,
how many times shall I forgive my brother or
sister who sins against me? Up to seven times?'
Jesus answered, 'I tell you, not seven
times, but seventy-seven times.'*

Matthew 18:21, 22

Have you ever exaggerated? Like, WAY beyond something reasonable? 'I could eat a horse' is one extreme addition we might make to another extreme statement: 'I am starving!' Generally speaking, neither of these are true – but we say them to make a point.

 Peter is being incredibly generous here! We can sometimes read this passage and think Peter has got fed up with someone and is looking for an excuse to punch their lights out – this is the fiery, quick to leap in, kind of Peter we expect. But, here Peter goes BEYOND what he would have been taught. Rabbis (Jewish teachers) would have advised three times as being sufficient to forgive someone, so Peter has gone DOUBLE on that with his suggestion.

 'Seventy-seven times.' This has also been understood to mean seventy times seven – which would then make 490 times! Essentially, a number so big that you would lose count – which is Jesus' point.

 The law, as far as Peter has understood it, means three times is sufficient, but hanging out with Jesus has led Peter to re-think that. He has seen Jesus forgive others in ways that have blown him away . . . BUT, what Peter imagines might be enough does not come close to the full measure of Jesus' grace and forgiveness!

 We can struggle to forgive. Maybe we struggle to forgive someone else who is a persistent pain in the neck. Maybe we struggle to forgive ourselves because we are constantly letting God down. We have here a glimpse – not just how far Jesus goes in his forgiveness – but, how far OUR forgiveness should go. Who do you need to forgive right now?

Day 17

*He came to Simon Peter, who said to him,
'Lord, are you going to wash my feet?' Jesus
replied, 'You do not realise now what I am
doing, but later you will understand.' 'No,'
said Peter, 'you shall never wash my feet.'*

John 13:6-8

Faith is upside down. We gain our life through Christ
by losing it, we become first by being last, and here the
King of kings becomes a servant.

 This was a disgusting job. Walking as they did
in dust, dirt, poo and muck, feet got absolutely
filthy. It would be the job of the lowest person in
a household to wash the feet of the guests. In this
context, the guest of honour, the most treasured
person at the table, the most honoured one, gets
the towel, gets down on his hands and knees,
picks up his disciples' stinking feet and begins
to wash them. No wonder then that Peter wants
none of it!

 'You do not realise now what I am doing.' Um,
yep – you have got that right! Peter doesn't have a
clue here. What does Jesus think he is doing? How
can this be?

Do you ever say *no* to Jesus? Think about the stink of your own messes and mistakes, think about the rank smell of those times you have lied or cheated or thought something awful – here comes Jesus, to wash it all away. No, Jesus, no!

 Saying *no* to Jesus is not just what we do when we are asked to do something hard – like be a missionary on the other side of the world or being kind to our brother or sister who is absolutely DOING OUR HEAD in! No, we can also reject what Jesus does when he makes us new and cleans us up, sets us right and brings us healing. We find it so hard sometimes to forgive ourselves for getting so dirty and messed up that we struggle to imagine Jesus dealing with it. But he does and he will – and if we are serious about being his followers – we must let him!

Day 18

Jesus answered, 'Unless I wash you, you have no part with me.' 'Then, Lord,' Simon Peter replied, 'not just my feet but my hands and my head as well!'

John 13:8, 9

Well, all right then – but don't stop there!! Have you ever been totally opposed to something, only to find yourself at a later point a total convert? When you REALISE something incredible about something you had dismissed, maybe?

 This is one of the reasons I love Peter! When Jesus basically says to him, 'That's it then Peter, if you won't let me wash your feet, we are DONE', Peter goes overboard. He so wants to be a part of what Jesus is doing. He doesn't want anything left out, nothing left to chance, no possibility of not being completely 'in' with Jesus! Peter does this more than once when something strikes him and he realises what is at stake.

 'My hands and my head as well!' When we are made clean by Jesus it is a work that happens on the inside, not the outside. The picture here is a symbol but Jesus wants Peter and the others to realise what they must do.

There is something else here, too. Jesus tells the disciples this is how they should be with each other. Servants. Preferring each other, looking to the needs of each other. Jesus knows he does not have long left with the disciples – we are properly approaching the cross now. They are going to need each other more than ever.

 Being a disciple, a follower of Jesus is not simply about you and him. Jesus does not call us to follow him in a vacuum, free of relationships with others. Who, right now, can you give thanks for – they share the journey, they share your load, they prefer and love you – as you try and prefer and love them? Give thanks for them now.

Day 19

*'You will all fall away,' Jesus told them, 'for
it is written: "I will strike the shepherd, and
the sheep will be scattered." But after I have
risen, I will go ahead of you into Galilee.' Peter
declared, 'Even if all fall away, I will not.*

Mark 14:27-29

Over these next few days of devotions we approach the
cross. We continue to look at Peter and his relationship
with Jesus, but this is where it gets really tough. It is
hard and painful for a while.

 Here, Jesus is quoting a powerful few words from
Zechariah chapter 13. Zechariah was written at
a time when Jerusalem was destroyed and the
temple in ruins. Here is Jesus, about to go to
the cross but, just as Zechariah finishes his book
with hope, Jesus brings encouragement with his
words, 'After I have risen, I will go ahead of you.'
At this point though, it seems as if Peter and the
others miss it.

 'Even if all fall away, I will not.' Peter. You have
got to love him. He really means this. He believes
what he says.

Have you ever promised something and then stuffed it up?

 Are we reliant on others to be with us all the time? Do we do what we do for Jesus because of the crowd, or because of what Jesus calls us to?

Day 20

Simon Peter asked him, 'Lord, where are you going?'
Jesus replied, 'Where I am going, you cannot
follow now, but you will follow later.' Peter asked,
'Lord, why can't I follow you now? I will lay
down my life for you.'

John 13:36, 37

Longing. Have you ever wanted something right now – but had to wait? Sometimes the waiting is good for us, but we don't appreciate it at the time.

 There is pain and confusion in what Peter is saying here. He does not understand what must happen, what must come next. 'You will follow later' could mean a couple of things here: 'Yes, Peter, you will also die like I am going to and will follow me there', or it could also be, 'You will be with me in my Father's house, in heaven, but you aren't coming just yet.'

 'Why can't I follow you now?' Now, please, I am done waiting! We live in this space between Jesus rising from the dead and going back to heaven and that glorious time to come when we will be with him where he is.

Sometimes, like Peter, we aren't ready for what is to come but we don't know it. This is why trusting Jesus is so important. He knows what we can and can't handle, what we are and what we are not ready for.

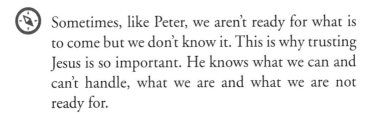 Wait. Even though you want to get up and go, wait. When you pray, sit still, take a quiet moment. Just wait a bit longer than normal today. KNOW that Jesus has gone before you.

Day 21

'Simon, Simon, Satan has asked to sift you as wheat. But I have prayed for you, Simon, that your faith may not fail. And when you have turned back, strengthen your brothers.'

Luke 22:31, 32

We do not fight alone. Whether it is in your head with your thoughts, your heart with your words, your hands and feet with your actions and where you go and what you do – we do not fight alone. We are prayed for and lifted up by Jesus himself! John 17 is Jesus' prayer for all of us (just as here, he tells Peter that he prays for him).

 We are jumping around a bit with this conversation. We started in Mark's Gospel and here is another snippet in Luke, not recorded by either Mark or Matthew in their accounts. When there is a narrative in the Gospels that is really important, get the whole picture by reading the different accounts. Just as if you and I witnessed something, different things would stand out for us, shock us, astound us or be etched on our memory. So it is with the Gospel accounts. It is just one reason they are so amazing. This is not a bunch of people trying to get their story straight – these are eye witness accounts, bringing out different aspects of what took place.

'When you have turned back, strengthen your brothers.' This is such an encouragement. Peter has not failed yet (we get to what he is going to do tomorrow) but Jesus knows it will happen and he is already being forgiven and given something important to do – before it has happened!

 There is nothing that can change the love that Jesus has for us. For you. Nothing. What you have done, what you will do. When we fail, when we fall, we are encouraged (as Peter is here) to strengthen others – nothing is wasted by God, not even our failings and faults.

 Who could you strengthen today? Maybe you don't feel up to it. Maybe that is just the time to press in and encourage, support or consider someone else. Right now. Who does God put on your heart as you are still right now? Who needs encouraging and strengthening?

Day 22

'Truly I tell you,' Jesus answered, 'today – yes,
tonight – before the cock crows twice you
yourself will have disowned me three times.'
But Peter insisted emphatically, 'Even if I have
to die with you, I will never disown you.'
And all the others said the same.

Mark 14:30, 31

Not a chance! Ever used big words to back something up only for something very small and maybe a bit rubbish to be the outcome? 'I will step forward and take the penalty, I never miss . . . oops', or 'Give it to me, I never have a problem opening jars – er, sorry, I smashed it', or 'I'll be there – I am NEVER late . . . um, I got held up, you know how it is.'

 There are some bits of the Bible where I see things for the first time. Seriously, it happens a lot and I have been reading it and studying it for years. There is NO END to what you will discover if you get stuck into the Bible. Writing these notes I have seen something here that I have never really noticed before – and it is this next bit under 'light bulb'.

 'All the others said the same.' Peter says out loud what everyone else is thinking and then they join in with a chorus of approval. It's not just Peter who is going to mess up and miss the mark here (and doesn't realise it), it's all of them. Every last one.

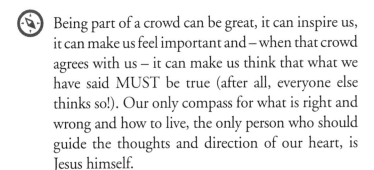

Being part of a crowd can be great, it can inspire us, it can make us feel important and – when that crowd agrees with us – it can make us think that what we have said MUST be true (after all, everyone else thinks so!). Our only compass for what is right and wrong and how to live, the only person who should guide the thoughts and direction of our heart, is Jesus himself.

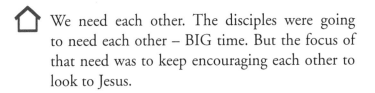

We need each other. The disciples were going to need each other – BIG time. But the focus of that need was to keep encouraging each other to look to Jesus.

Day 23

They went to a place called Gethsemane, and Jesus said to his disciples, 'Sit here while I pray.' He took Peter, James and John along with him, and he began to be deeply distressed and troubled. 'My soul is overwhelmed with sorrow to the point of death,' he said to them. 'Stay here and keep watch.

Mark 14:32-34

Ever been in on something that you wished you weren't? Anything from a slightly embarrassing conversation to something that you witness or see and don't know what to do with yourself – it all just feels too hard and painful to take in?

 We are getting to the tough stuff. Jesus knows what is coming and he doesn't go all macho in front of his disciples, 'The Cross – HA! a mere trifle.' Jesus gets serious and honest with his closest friends – this is the hardest thing he has ever done. Suddenly, Peter, James and John get a window on the painful reality of what is in store for Jesus.

 'Stay here and keep watch.' A watchman was someone who looked for the enemy, who often kept watch until the morning, making sure things were safe, ready to raise the alarm.

At times, things are not amazing in our lives. Jesus goes to pray and he is deeply distressed, troubled and overwhelmed. It is ok to feel like this when we pray. Jesus did. Jesus knows what it feels like to have nothing left and be almost despairing.

 When you pray, make it real with God – just as Jesus did in front of Peter, James and John. God knows what is really happening in our lives and hearts – so it doesn't do us any good to pretend we are 'fine'. Be real now. Pray now.

Day 24

Then he returned to his disciples and found them sleeping. 'Simon', he said to Peter, 'are you asleep? Couldn't you watch and pray for one hour? Watch and pray that you do not fall into temptation. The spirit is willing, but the flesh is weak.'

Mark 14:37, 38

It is pretty classic to nod off when we are praying. If we are exhausted, had a 'day', feeling hungry, angry, lonely, tired ... Then we are expected to pray?

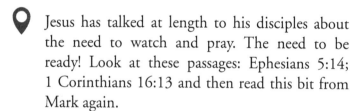 Jesus has talked at length to his disciples about the need to watch and pray. The need to be ready! Look at these passages: Ephesians 5:14; 1 Corinthians 16:13 and then read this bit from Mark again.

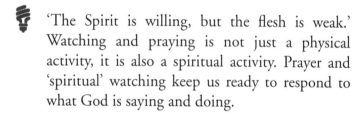 'The Spirit is willing, but the flesh is weak.' Watching and praying is not just a physical activity, it is also a spiritual activity. Prayer and 'spiritual' watching keep us ready to respond to what God is saying and doing.

We are in a battle. It is a spiritual battle – not a physical one, but a spiritual one. A battle for our hearts and minds. Paul writes about it in Romans

7:14-25. This is why we must pray, this is why we must be watchful . . . we cannot sleepwalk through our lives as Christians!

 Have you nodded off in your Christian faith? Do you need to wake up? Ask God's Holy Spirit to help you today.

Day 25

Then Simon Peter, who had a sword, drew it and struck the high priest's servant, cutting off his right ear. Jesus commanded Peter, 'Put your sword away! Shall I not drink the cup the Father has given me?'

John 18:10, 11

There has got to be another way! Let's use our brute strength or our brain or our looks to get there.

 Nothing explains to us why Peter has a sword. Maybe he sensed trouble, but it is mostly an illustration of how much he has still to understand about Jesus and the kingdom. He knows Jesus is King, he has declared Jesus as Lord, but Peter's lack of understanding about what those things look like lead to this violent episode.

 'Shall I not drink the cup the Father has given me?' 'The cup' is Jesus' reference here to the sacrifice he is going to make. Going to the cross HAS to happen. Jesus must die.

 Do we fully understand who Jesus is? Peter declared him Lord and Messiah. He got a pat on the back and discovered some things about himself in the process, as we have already seen in an early reading. Yet he still hasn't grasped HOW Jesus is going to accomplish what he has come to do.

 We might say Jesus is Lord, but Lord of what, and Lord how? In what way? Where is Jesus' kingdom at work in our lives? Are we fully his? In so many ways we continue to learn and discover more about Jesus' love, grace, power and presence in our lives – I am still discovering things. Even as I have been writing these notes, I have learnt so much! What might Jesus have for you to discover about him today?

Day 26

Simon Peter and another disciple were following Jesus. Because this disciple was known to the high priest, he went with Jesus into the high priest's courtyard, but Peter had to wait outside at the door. The other disciple came back, who was known to the high priest, spoke to the servant-girl on duty there and brought Peter in. 'You aren't one of this man's disciples too, are you?' she asked Peter. He replied, 'I am not.' It was cold, and the servants and officials stood round a fire they had made to keep warm. Peter also was standing with them, warming himself.

John 18:15-18

Here we are then. We reach the first of Peter's denials. Have you ever been asked, 'Are you his friend?' and you have replied, 'I am not?'

 Where it says 'following Jesus', it feels ironic here as we are considering what it looks like to 'follow Jesus'. Here it feels embarrassing, they don't want to be associated too closely with Jesus, but they want to know what is happening. Peter has to wait outside. What must those few seconds, minutes have been like?

'You aren't one of this man's disciples too, are you?' This could be said with a whole host of different tones. We don't get that from reading it. It might have been, 'Not another one!', or it could have been, 'Surely not, you don't look like one of his followers!' What does a Jesus follower look like anyway?

 You may never have felt like denying Jesus with a strong, 'I am not' his friend, but we can just as easily deny him with silence, or deny him by joining in with a rude joke, or laughing with the crowd at someone who is being bullied. Do we feel mortified if someone thinks we are a follower of Jesus or do we feel thrilled that they might have noticed?

 The rubber hits the road for us, just as it did for Peter, when he was not surrounded by an adoring crowd (think of how easy it can feel to be a Christian in a big worship event) but by people openly hostile to Jesus and what he was doing. Pray now for peace and courage to stand for Jesus when it is easy – and when it is hard.

Day 27

Simon Peter was still standing there warming himself. So they asked him, 'You aren't one of his disciples too, are you?' He denied it, saying, 'I am not.' One of the high priest's servants, a relative of the man whose ear Peter had cut off, challenged him, 'Didn't I see you with him in the garden?' Again Peter denied it, and at that moment a cock began to crow.

John 18:25-27

Keep digging mate, no point stopping now. Yes, I know it is getting worse but what else are you going to do?

 In the narrative we have jumped between Peter's first denial and then these two further denials. The skip was to see what Jesus was facing, then it's back to Peter. It is a powerful contrast. Jesus composed and calm, Peter shaken and getting cross and digging a bigger hole for himself – especially as there seems to be an eye witness who spotted him in the garden.

 'Didn't I see you with him in the garden?' Wow, this is a gut punch for Peter – someone saw him in the garden! Saw what a mess he had made of things. He hadn't stayed awake and prayed, he hadn't kept his cool (instead he had attacked someone) and here he is, losing his cool again. Will this night never end? Then the cock crows.

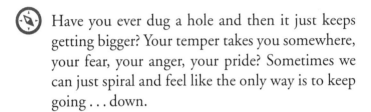 Have you ever dug a hole and then it just keeps getting bigger? Your temper takes you somewhere, your fear, your anger, your pride? Sometimes we can just spiral and feel like the only way is to keep going . . . down.

Are we sad when we fail Jesus because we fail Jesus or because we get found out? It doesn't tell us here what Peter felt or thought when someone said, 'But, I SAW you!' We can't be caught in the act with Jesus – because he knows all there is to know. Confessing our sin is not for his benefit – he knows what we have done. It is for ours, to come clean, to own up, to say it like it really is. Take a moment, then a deep breath – and tell Jesus something you have been holding back on.

Day 28

The Lord turned and looked straight at Peter.
Then Peter remembered the word that the Lord
had spoken to him: 'Before the cock crows today,
you will disown me three times.' And he
went outside and wept bitterly.

Luke 22:61, 62

A look can say a lot. A look from a teacher across the classroom, a look from a boyfriend or a girlfriend (that only the two people gazing into each other's eyes understand!). A look from a friend when you have let them down.

 What is hard to imagine, and yet seems clear from the story here, is that Jesus is being interrogated within the sight and earshot of Peter. Peter has had his OWN interrogation, the fate of the world does not rest on it, but he has failed it all the same.

 'He went outside and wept bitterly.' Now it comes back to him, now he sees what he has done, the full extent of it. Maybe Peter also remembers all his fine words at this point (I will never leave you, the rest might but not me, I would never deny you, I would die for you, not me Lord, NEVER!).

We might sometimes do things that we consider are so bad that there is no way back. 'I should have known better', we might think. 'I DID know better ... but I messed up anyway.' Missing the mark is literally what the word sin means. Sometimes it feels as if we have forgotten there IS a mark.

 What you have done, however bad it seems, has already been dealt with. The price for it has already been paid. Jesus went to the cross BECAUSE this stuff happens. In fact, Paul says that while we were still missing the mark, far off from God – Christ died for us (Romans 5:8). Say sorry now. Say thank you now.

Day 29

So Peter and the other disciple started for the tomb. Both were running, but the other disciple outran Peter and reached the tomb first. He bent over and looked in at the strips of linen lying there but did not go in. Then Simon Peter came along behind him and went straight into the tomb.

John 20:3-6

We have jumped from that awful moment for Peter to one of astonishment for Peter – he isn't really mentioned in between. The focus has been on the cross and on Jesus' suffering. What is taking place in Peter's life is out of view until he arrives, breathless at the tomb.

 The context here is they have just heard unbelievable news. Of Jesus' closest followers only two head for the tomb and, obviously, one of them is Peter. Peter doesn't get there first, but he notices the other disciple doesn't go in. Peter though, being Peter, rushes straight past and into the tomb!

 'Both were running.' This is just a simple thought, but sometimes there is an urgency about the gospel, about the good news – this was the most amazing news EVER. Whether they believed it or not when they set off, they RAN. Why? Because of …excitement, fear, a growing sense of joy that they couldn't quite take hold of until they got there?

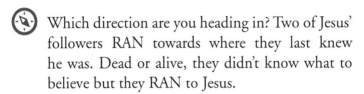 Which direction are you heading in? Two of Jesus' followers RAN towards where they last knew he was. Dead or alive, they didn't know what to believe but they RAN to Jesus.

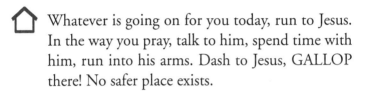 Whatever is going on for you today, run to Jesus. In the way you pray, talk to him, spend time with him, run into his arms. Dash to Jesus, GALLOP there! No safer place exists.

Day 30

But they did not believe the women, because their words seemed to them like nonsense. Peter, however, got up and ran to the tomb. Bending over, he saw the strips of linen lying by themselves, and he went away, wondering to himself what had happened.

Luke 24:11, 12

Seeing is believing! Someone tells you about a stonking video clip of something amazing on youtube. You see for yourself – but, in this age of ridiculous special effects, do we even believe what we see? Is it real? Paul says that if Jesus did not rise from the dead then we are bonkers (1 Corinthians 15:14).

 The women were the first to receive the news of Jesus' resurrection. At that time, a woman's testimony was not valid in a court of law by itself, unless a man had also witnessed what they had. Yes, pretty rubbish I know, but as well as the disciples still not grasping that Jesus was going to rise from the dead, they now had to get their heads round the witness of some women. But this cultural challenge does not stop Peter . . . off he goes!

'Bending over, he saw the strips of linen lying by themselves.' That might seem an odd verse to focus on, but Peter goes and sees with his own eyes, he looks in and takes in the scene. The tomb is open. No body. What the body would have been wrapped in just lying there. Do we, like Peter, need to see with our own eyes? Do we believe the witness of others? What is it that means we 'believe' even when we have not seen?

 You and I were not there when Jesus died and rose again, but the Gospels are so vivid, with so many details from the Last Supper to Gethsemane, to the cross, to the tomb and beyond. The greatest event in history was also something that happened at a certain moment in time with people – people just like us – struggling to come to terms with what was going on. Peter was just one of those.

 We are also part of the great story. We are in what we understand as the age of the Spirit (we will get to this in some readings to come). But as we are part of God's family now, we are linked with Peter and all those who have come since . . . ALL the followers of Jesus, part of the family of God. Part of OUR family. Part of OUR story. Wow!

Day 31

*'I'm going out to fish,' Simon Peter told them, and
they said, 'We'll go with you.' So they went out
and got into the boat, but that night they caught
nothing. Early in the morning, Jesus stood on the
shore, but the disciples did not realise it was Jesus.*

John 21:3, 4

Well, that's it then. All done. Back to what we know.
Safety of things we can do REALLY well – oh, we can't
even do this any more!!

 I don't know WHAT is going through the disciples'
minds at this point. Jesus has risen from the dead
– they know this. They have seen him. The bit
before these verses says that Jesus did many more
miraculous signs in front of his disciples. But even
with all that going on, Peter goes back to what
is familiar, to what is safe, to what he can get his
head around. He goes fishing.

 'I'm going out to fish.' This is not the fishing
that Jesus had in mind. Remember, Jesus HAS
appeared to the disciples . . . but has said nothing
to Peter yet about what he did – denying he even
knew Jesus. Maybe Peter thinks he is done being
a disciple. Maybe Peter thinks that JESUS thinks
he is done being a disciple.

Have you ever thought that? Jesus is looking at you with disappointment in his eyes. 'You have really let me down,' they say. When we feel we are out of sorts with Jesus it can be a tough time, but we don't make it any easier by pretending everything is normal (our equivalent of just heading off to fish like nothing has happened).

 This is called the 'Home' icon. Our place of home is with Jesus, but sometimes we can feel miles away from him because of thoughts, words or actions that have become a wedge between us and him. Come home right now. Turn round right now. Look up to Jesus rather than down at your feet. Know that he loves and cherishes you right now.

Day 32

Then the disciple whom Jesus loved said to Peter,
'It is the Lord!' As soon as Simon Peter heard him
say, 'It is the Lord,' he wrapped his outer garment
around him (for he had taken it off) and jumped
into the water. The other disciples followed in the
boat, towing the net full of fish, for they were not
far from the shore, about a hundred yards.

John 21:7, 8

Stuff this! There is Jesus – what am I doing here?

 Jesus does it again. The guy who isn't a fisherman shows them how it is done. They can achieve NOTHING without Jesus – even, it seems, what they could do before they met him (unless they were just always pretty rubbish at fishing). Peter is so desperate to see Jesus that he leaps out of what was probably his own boat, leaving the others to drag in the fish. No walking on water – just straight in!

 'It is the Lord!' Someone else needs to say it, but when Peter realises, then nothing else matters. He doesn't care what the others think about him leaping out of the boat as he does, half-swimming, half-wading to the shore. All he can think, all he can see is, 'It is the Lord!'

Sometimes Jesus so FILLS our view that we can see nothing else. Even with what is hanging over Peter, his guilt and his shame, he dashes TO Jesus rather than hides away from him. What do we do when we feel like that?

 What FILLS your vision today? If the Lord were to appear – at the bottom of your bed rather than on the seashore, but right there, within reach – would you rush towards him or shrink away? How do you feel about seeing him today – in the lives of others, in your own actions and habits, words and thoughts . . .

Day 33

*Jesus said, 'Feed my sheep. I tell you the truth,
when you were younger you dressed yourself and
went where you wanted; but when you are old
you will stretch out your hands, and someone
else will dress you and lead you where you do
not want to go.' Jesus said this to indicate the
kind of death by which Peter would glorify God.
Then he said to him, 'Follow me!'*

John 21:17-19

Haven't we been here before? Sometimes life with God can feel like we are living something all over again, maybe we even feel like we are right back at the start.

 What comes before this passage is a brief conversation where Jesus reminds Peter of what he has done in denying him, by asking him three times, 'Do you love me?' The first two times Jesus uses the word *agape*, which is about preferring and loving unconditionally. Peter, in his replies, uses the word *phileo*, which is like the love of a friend (Do you love me? Well, I like you a lot . . .) Jesus is trying to help Peter understand the kind of love Peter will need to follow him and do the things he will have to do. Jesus indicates it is going to get tough for Peter, who is going to need to love Jesus more than just a friend.

'Follow me!' This is pretty much where we started with Peter, but we are not back at the beginning – loads has happened in between the first call to follow and this one. It is a call we might receive many times ourselves in our journey with Jesus.

 This icon is called 'compass', as I have tried to explore what our direction is, which way we are going. When we first become followers of Jesus, we arrive at the cross and we realise what he has done for us. As we journey with Jesus, we continue to arrive at the cross again and again, for we need constant reminders of who Jesus is and what he has done for us. The call to follow is part of Jesus' encouragement, welcome and acceptance of Peter as his disciple. When we see the cross and see Jesus, we are reminded of his great love and great grace as we journey onwards.

 Starting again with Jesus is not about going back to the beginning. It is, though, a chance to be forgiven (again), cleansed (again), filled (again) and get fired up for the journey ahead. No matter HOW many times we find ourselves back at the cross, it is always to help us move forward in our life with God. Listen again and hear Jesus say, 'Do you love me?' Start moving again as you hear Jesus say, 'Follow me!'

Day 34

*In those days Peter stood up among the believers
(a group numbering about a hundred and
twenty) and said, 'Brothers and sisters, the
scripture had to be fulfilled which the Holy
Spirit spoke long ago through the mouth of
David concerning Judas, who served as a guide
for those who arrested Jesus – he was one of
our number and shared in this ministry.'*

Acts 1:15-17

Sometimes there is a time to make a stand or take a stand
or just do something. You can't be a passive observer,
something must be done!

 Just before these verses Jesus has been taken up
to heaven and the disciples returned to Jerusalem.
They met together in constant prayer. It is out
of this atmosphere of prayer and seeking God
that Peter stands up and speaks. The numbers of
Jesus' followers was larger than the 12 disciples
and it is this larger group that is gathered when
Peter speaks. He seems to speak here with a
new authority, with a sense of purpose. Maybe
he is beginning to 'follow' in the way Jesus was
encouraging him to do.

'Peter stood up.' Someone had to take the lead and it was Peter. All that he is and all that Jesus saw in Peter when he called him a 'Rock' is beginning to take shape around what Jesus called him to. Feed my sheep, was his instruction to Peter at the end of John's Gospel and here he is, explaining the scriptures, using God's word to lead the followers of Jesus forward.

 What do you stand for? What gets you on your feet? What moves you to action? It is important to consider this – God made you, through and through. Your likes, passions, hopes and dreams are part of an amazing creation called 'you'. When we give our whole selves to Jesus, as Peter was realising he had to do, then we can do anything for Jesus.

 Taking a stand begins with little things. Peter had three years with Jesus as a friend and follower. Jesus was his example, his model and his Lord.

Day 35

Then Peter stood up with the Eleven, raised his voice and addressed the crowd: 'Fellow Jews and all of you who live in Jerusalem, let me explain this to you; listen carefully to what I say. These men are not drunk, as you suppose. It is only nine in the morning! No, this is what was spoken by the prophet Joel.'

Acts 2:14-16

Being inspired by the Spirit, being filled by the Spirit and being asked to do something by the Spirit can be nerve-shredding! At the same time it can be amazing to know that as we speak or act, the Spirit is enabling us. We know at those times that we cannot do what we are doing! The only way we can be doing it is with God's help.

 A lot of background to what is happening here. First, this 'preach' from Peter is happening at Pentecost. For the Jews this is the festival of 'weeks', marking a seven week period from when the Passover happens to when the law is received on Mount Sinai. (You can check those out in the Old Testament.) Jerusalem is FULL of Jews from all over who have come for the festival. The disciples have just been filled with the Spirit and people are thinking they are drunk – maybe because this festival is a bit of a party, a bit of a celebration. The Jews are celebrating the gift of the law; today we celebrate Pentecost as the time we received the gift of the Holy Spirit.

 'This is what was spoken by the Prophet Joel.' Here, Peter quotes from an Old Testament prophet, go and give it a read here: Joel 2:28-32.

 Our guide, as it was for the disciples, is scripture. The disciples lived alongside Jesus and saw him do amazing things, but they also heard him refer to and rely on scripture. Jesus did what he did in keeping with scripture and he understood it like nobody else. Here, Peter relies on it; he sees (as the Holy Spirit shows him) the link between what Joel said would happen and what was happening right then. If we are going to take seriously Jesus' calling us to 'follow', we must read, study, enjoy, know and be inspired by his Word. The Bible is our map, the Holy Spirit is our guide, being more like Jesus is our destination!

 This is day 35 on our journey. This might be the only time you have got stuck into the Bible for a few weeks at a time. Cool isn't it! I have learned loads putting these devotions together – but please, don't stop at the end of this book. The Bible leads us to a place of goodness and peace, as we rest in God's word, read the story of God's people (who are also OUR people!), trust in the promises we find here . . . there is so MUCH more than the little we have explored.

Day 36

Now a man crippled from birth was being carried to the temple gate called Beautiful, where he was put every day to beg from those going into the temple courts. When he saw Peter and John about to enter, he asked them for money. Peter looked straight at him, as did John. Then Peter said, 'Look at us!' So the man gave them his attention, expecting something from them.

Acts 3:2-5

Have you ever wanted someone to look at you and really see you? Look at me! It is the kind of thing little children shout when they are doing something cool ... 'Look at me!! Look what I can do, look what I can draw, look, look, look ...'

 A good time to be at the temple was at prayer time. That was when people were going in and out – a GREAT time to beg if you had nothing. In Peter and John's day, if you were ill or sick, you were considered to be unclean. The gate where this man often sat was called 'Beautiful' – the unclean, rejected and despised sitting outside at the beautiful gate. Read on to the end of verse 10.

'Look at us!' Peter and John tell the man to look at them, not because they have something, but so that he can see that they have nothing. Nothing of themselves that they can give, no money that will ease this man's suffering (but not take it away). They have something more amazing and they give him what they have – in the name of Jesus!

 You may be cool. It may be that people look at you and think, 'Wow, he/she is SO amazing.' It may be that you think people look straight through you and don't see you at all. Peter and John had nothing as far as the world was concerned – no money, no power, no status. They weren't the most popular kids, they didn't 'have it all'. They had given what they had to follow Jesus, and now they were giving to this man from what Jesus had given them.

 When we pray, whether it is for someone to be healed or that we have a good day or that we might be more patient etc., we don't then answer our own prayer by trying to be a better person or make something happen. We are praying and asking God to come, asking God to heal, asking God to grow his fruit in our lives. Without him we can do nothing. Peter and John knew this, but do we know this? Do we live totally reliant on God?

Day 37

Then they called them in again and commanded them not to speak or teach at all in the name of Jesus. But Peter and John replied, 'Judge for yourselves whether it is right in God's sight to obey you rather than God. For we cannot help speaking about what we have seen and heard.'

Acts 4:18-20

You do a good thing, an amazing thing maybe! God has been with you, something stunning has happened and you feel pretty good – then it gets a bit rubbish. Not EVERYONE is happy about it.

 Peter says something amazing in the verses before this, the Holy Spirit is particularly mentioned because we are to take particular notice of it. In verse 12 Peter says, 'Salvation is found in no one else, for there is no other name under heaven given to men by which we must be saved.' BOOM. The 'no one else' Peter is talking about is Jesus, and these two – Peter and John – are in serious trouble. They have been doing what Jesus had been doing! Healing people and sharing the good news! They are, in this passage, before the religious leaders to explain themselves. 'How can you be doing this?' It is only by the power of God (as we saw yesterday) and they do not CARE what others might say or do, they WILL do what Jesus has called them to do.

 'For we cannot help speaking': Having talked about being willing to stand up for Jesus, Peter is now speaking for Jesus with the help of the Holy Spirit, and he cannot HELP it. He must do it! Jesus has so transformed his life that he does not fear the threats made, he does not seek the popularity of others, he does not worry about the future.

 We may not find ourselves in extreme circumstances but when Peter was squeezed and pressured and threatened, what came out of him? Words inspired by the Holy Spirit. When we are squeezed or pressured or threatened, what comes out of us? How we respond when things are tough is a mark of our trust and our hope in God, not in our circumstances.

 We are on the last lap, a few days to go! Maybe you can think of times when you have stood up, but have been unable to speak or been unsure what to say. Maybe pray today that if that chance comes again, the Holy Spirit will give you the words to say, as he did with Peter.

Day 38

'Surely not, Lord!' Peter replied. 'I have never eaten anything impure or unclean.' The voice spoke to him a second time, 'Do not call anything impure that God has made clean.'

Acts 10:14, 15

Do you have a log in your eye? Something that blocks your view? Do you have a blind spot where your own prejudice or a strongly-held view stops you seeing things the way God wants you to see them?

 There is LOADS to read either side of these verses – read the whole of chapter 10 to get the full picture. In a nutshell, Peter is struggling to accept those who are not Jews as fellow believers and followers of Jesus. They don't eat the same things, they don't act the same, they don't follow the Jewish laws. (Most early Christians were Jews, until the Good News began to spread – especially through the missionary work of Paul.) What is interesting and encouraging to me is that just before this passage where Peter is struggling, he has raised someone from the dead! Just because we are used by God to do mighty things does not mean we are not still learning and discovering new things about what Jesus is doing and wants to do. Peter has to deal with his issue about those who are not Jews and welcome them into God's big family.

 'Surely not, Lord!' Do we know better than God? Sometimes I think I have such confidence I could tell God a thing or two! 'You can't mean that, Lord. You wouldn't do that, Lord. Maybe you'd better let me handle this, Jesus, you seem to be off your game.' Peter had a fixed view and he is taking time to budge and get what Jesus is saying.

 Do you need to budge from a position you hold? It might be something small – you don't like the fact there are new people in the youth group, this isn't the way songs should be sung, that person over there prayers in the wrong way – THEY can't be a Christian, can they? Maybe there is a log in your eye. You can't see what Jesus wants you to see because YOU have decided how things are.

 Ask God to open up your heart and mind, to give you eyes to see things the way he sees them. Ask him to show you where there might be prejudice and wrong-thinking and pray for a right and Jesus-centred attitude today.

Day 39

Praise be to the God and Father of our Lord Jesus Christ! In his great mercy he has given us new birth into a living hope through the resurrection of Jesus Christ from the dead, and into an inheritance that can never perish, spoil or fade. This inheritance is kept in heaven for you.

1 Peter 1:3, 4

We zip for our last two days to Peter's letters, written about the same time as the book of Acts. Peter has been doing some AMAZING things for Jesus – what a turnaround – and he wants to SHARE with others all that God has shown him.

 This is the opening of Peter's first letter in the New Testament. We think it was written some time in the early AD 60s, so probably about 30 years after Jesus had ascended into heaven. Peter wrote it to encourage the scattered Church, to remind them to persevere and to be a witness to the Good News, so that nobody could say anything bad about them.

 'a living hope': These are precious words for those Peter is writing to. Things are tough for the early Church. There has been persecution, there are people who aren't teaching the truth and are speaking of things that are not good news. Peter reminds his readers to focus on the living hope – Jesus himself.

 What do you hope in? What is your hope as we draw to the end of these readings? Where are you storing up your treasure – in this life? Or, in a place where it will not go rotten, break, become obsolete (be upgraded as soon as you have bought it!), where the latest trend does not matter more than your closest friend (that's Jesus, by the way).

 Pray that Jesus would be your hope and your joy. Whatever might come, that you could fix your eyes, your dreams, your ambition on the things of God – that Jesus would be your peace and your assurance of a perfect home to come.

Day 40

So I will always remind you of these things,
even though you know them and are firmly
established in the truth you now have. I think it
is right to refresh your memory as long as I live
in the tent of this body, because I know that I
will soon put it aside, as our Lord Jesus Christ
has made clear to me. And I will make every
effort to see that after my departure you will
always be able to remember these things.

2 Peter 1:12-15

If you could only share a few things with people about Jesus and then that was it, what would you share? What would they need to know?

 This is near the beginning of Peter's final letter. He is getting things in order and sharing what MUST be shared. Peter is never one to hold back and he doesn't in this letter. It is full of passion, persuasion, encouragement, challenge and love. He talks about memory, being reminded and remembering three times in these verses. He himself is remembering what Jesus said to him 30 years earlier, as he recalls how Jesus said he would die.

'refresh your memory': What Peter is doing here is encouraging his readers to recall a good memory by the inspiration of the Holy Spirit. Keep in mind, don't forget, keep remembering!

 I think we can all too easily remember the bad stuff, remember the rotten stuff and let that be our abiding memory of things. Peter, like you and me, has stuff in his life he could recall and it would not be good. He does not do that here! His JOY is to think about, reflect on and remember Jesus. To know him AGAIN, by continuing to focus on Jesus' promises, presence and devotion to us that led him to the cross – and the power of God that raised him (and us) to new life!

 We are here, we've reached our last thought on Peter's journey with Jesus. Let your mind, heart and soul be refreshed and renewed as you recall and remember the life, death and resurrection of Jesus our Saviour, who calls us, along with Peter and so many countless others, as he says, 'Follow me!'